PRIMARY SOURCES TEACHING KIT

Explorers

by Karen Baicker

SCHOLASTIC PROFESSIONAL BOOKS

New York • Toronto • London • Auckland • Sydney
Mexico City • New Delhi • Hong Kong • Buenos Aires

for Keith Baicker

COVER DOCUMENTS: Archivo General de Indias, Seville: Treaty of Tordesillas; **The Mariner's Museum,** Newport News, VA: drawing of Magellan's ship *The Victoria*; **North Wind Picture Archives,** Alfred, ME: map from *Ptolemy's Geography*, sea serpent engraving

INTERIOR DOCUMENTS: American Museum of Natural History, New York, NY: 43 [Neg. #286821]; **Archivo de la Corona de Aragon,** Barcelona, ES: 25; **Archivo General de Indias,** Seville: 34; **Beinecke Library, Yale University,** New Haven, CT: 20; **Biblioteca Colombina,** Sevilla, ES: 23, 24; **Houghton Library, Harvard University,** Cambridge, MA: 35; **Library of Congress,** 27 (center and right) [LC-USZ62 39304]; 30; **The Mariners Museum,** Newport News, VA: 18, 32 (right), 33 (top), 36; **National Maritime Museum,** Greenwich, London: 33 (bottom); **North Wind Picture Archives,** Alfred, ME: 21 (top and bottom), 22, 24, 28 (right and left), 29, 31, 32 (left), 37, 38, 40, 41

Ptolemy's World Map, page 46, originally appeared in *Mapman's Guide to Understanding Your World* (Scholastic, 2002). Used with permission.

Edited by Sean Price
Picture research by Dwayne Howard
Cover design by Norma Ortiz
Interior design and illustration by Melinda Belter
Map, page 46, by Jim McMahon
ISBN: 0-590-37865-1

Contents

INTRODUCTION

Using Primary Sources in the Classroom

The Age of Exploration offers some of the earliest primary sources available regarding our country. The documents—woodcuts, old hand-drawn maps, illustrations of ships, journal entries—reveal much more than the facts of explorers' brave journeys. They suggest what life was like during this exciting time in world history.

Primary sources offer a wealth of other benefits for your students as well. Textbooks often present a single interpretation of events; primary sources compel the reader to supply his or her own interpretation. A thoughtful analysis of primary sources requires both basic and advanced critical thinking skills: classifying documents, determining point of view, evaluating bias, comparing and contrasting, and reading for detail.

Primary sources can also help students recognize that the artifacts of our contemporary lives—a ticket stub, a school report card, a yearbook—may one day be fodder for future historians.

One of the most important steps in teaching history is to help students understand the difference between primary and secondary sources. Share the chart below to demonstrate the categories to your class.

MATERIAL	DEFINITION	EXAMPLES
Primary Sources	Documents created during or immediately following the event they describe, by people who had firsthand knowledge of the event	Letters, diaries, photographs, artifacts, newspaper articles, paintings
Secondary Sources	Documents created by people who were not present at the event that occurred	History books, biographies, newspaper articles

Keep a folder handy with copies of the primary source evaluation form on page 17. Encourage students to complete the reproducible as they study each document in this book. Eventually, this kind of analysis will be automatic for your students as they encounter primary sources in their future studies.

Using The Internet to Find Primary Sources

The Internet can be an amazing tool for finding primary sources. Just remind your students that extra care has to be taken in verifying that the source is reliable. Here are a few outstanding sites for using primary sources in the classroom:

Library of Congress: **http://www.loc.gov**

National Archives Records Administration: **http://www.nara.gov**

Eduplace: **http://www.eduplace.com/ss/hmss/primary.html**

The Avalon Project: **http://www.yale.edu/lawweb/avalon/avalon.htm**

Internet Archive of Texts and Documents: **http://history.hanover.edu/texts.htm**

Ask your students to find other great sites for primary sources and create their own list. Keep a running list handy, posted near a computer terminal.

Background on the Age of Exploration (c.1001–1778)

The Age of Exploration is also sometimes called The Age of Discovery, and the distinction between the terms belies one of the major issues in teaching this time period. For, as social studies teachers and others now hasten to point out, when the explorers reached the Americas they were not discovering a "new world" that was previously unknown. There were Native Americans whose ancestors had been living there for thousands of years. And the ensuing encounters wreaked havoc on their way of life, essentially destroying their existence within the era.

So, teaching about the explorers has become a delicate topic. How do we acknowledge the tremendous challenges, achievements, and impact of the explorers while respecting the terrible consequences as well? One answer is through primary sources. But with this topic it is essential to emphasize that just because a source is "primary" does not mean it is accurate. Many of these documents provide excellent opportunities to analyze point of view and look for bias. The explorers' descriptions of the Native Americans they encountered, the maps rife with errors and distortions, the illustrations seen from a slanted view, all reveal the collective knowledge and perspective of the time.

It is now known that, contrary to common belief only decades ago, Columbus was not the first person to discover America. The continent has been "discovered" many different times—first, by the wandering hunters crossing the land bridge in prehistoric times, then by the Vikings from Greenland whose sagas relate their history, then by Columbus, and then by waves of explorers from different European countries. In a sense, the exploration of America has continued ever since, by waves of immigrants who cross the same ocean to start new adventures.

Two worlds that had existed separately for thousands of years—Europe and the Americas—were at once and forever connected. The great exchange began, and continues.

About This Book

Focusing primarily on the period beginning with Columbus and ending around 1600, the documents that follow offer an overview of the age of exploration and speak to these questions: Why do people explore? What was going on in Europe at the time? What was life like on the seas? What happened from a cultural perspective when the explorers arrived?

This collection helps you teach students to use primary source materials and to think critically about the Age of Exploration. Your students will benefit most from working with these documents when you help to set a context and engage them with critical viewing and thinking activities. Students can prepare for a discussion about any of the documents in this collection by studying the document and completing the student reproducible Evaluate That Document! (page 17). This primary source evaluation form guides students to identify important document characteristics and pose questions prior to the class discussion. Feel free to reproduce this form as you need it.

The Teaching Notes section provides background information and teaching suggestions for each document. Reproducible pages for the activity suggestions can be found at the back of the book.

Several documents, such as Columbus's letter to Louis de Santangel (page 30), feature text that is written not only in another language, but also in an early form of that language. For these documents, we have included typeset translations along with the original document. This way, students can understand these sources as actual, physical documents, and as meaningful texts. Illustrative secondary sources including the images on pages 18, 37, 38, 40, and 41 are paired with typeset materials to help provide a visual context for these documents.

Time Line of the Age of Exploration

(c. 1001–1778)

1001 The Viking Leif Eriksson reaches Newfoundland

1492 The Spanish king and queen, Ferdinand and Isabella, conquer Granada, the last Muslim kingdom on the Iberian Peninsula

1492 Christopher Columbus, under the flag of Spain, makes his first voyage west across the Atlantic Ocean and reaches the islands of the Caribbean on October 12

1493 Columbus makes his second voyage and establishes a settlement on the Island of Hispaniola

1494 Spain and Portugal sign The Treaty of Tordesillas, which divides the New World between the two countries

1497 Sailing under the English flag, the Italian John Cabot reaches Newfoundland off the coast of North America

1498 Columbus reaches the coast of South America on his third voyage

1500–1513 Numerous Spanish sea captains scour the Caribbean and the coast of Central America in search of a way further west

1507 The first map is published in which the New World is called America

1510 The Spanish bring the first African slaves to the Americas

1513 The Spaniard Ponce de Leon discovers and names Florida

1513 Traveling through the Isthmus of Panama, Vasco Nuñez de Balboa discovers the Pacific Ocean and claims it for Spain

1519–1522 Sailing for the Spanish, the Portuguese navigator Ferdinand Magellan circumnavigates the globe

1519 Mexico is conquered for Spain when Hernando Cortéz defeats the Aztec ruler Montezuma

1524 Sailing for France, Giovanni da Verrazano explores the coast of North America in search of a strait to China

1534 Frenchman Jacques Cartier explores the St. Lawrence River in Canada

1542 Portuguese Juan Cabrillo explores the coast of California for Spain

1576–1610 Numerous explorers, including the Englishmen Martin Frobisher and Henry Hudson search for a northwest passage to China in the Bays of Hudson and Baffin in northern Canada

1577 Sir Francis Drake explores the west coast of North America

1607 English colony of Jamestown, Virginia is settled

1624 Dutch settle the colony of New Amsterdam. Upon its surrender to the English in 1664, the colony is renamed New York

1778 After discovering the Hawaiian Islands, the British Captain James Cook maps the Pacific coastline of North America as far north as the Arctic Circle

EXPLORATION BEFORE COLUMBUS

The Vinland Sagas: c. 1000 A.D.

Use with pages 18–19.

BACKGROUND

Although many of us and all of our parents were taught that Columbus discovered America, it is now known that the Vikings landed in America half a millennium before Columbus's famous voyage.

The Vikings began sailing west in the 800s searching for new land to conquer. Erik the Red reached Greenland. Later, his son, Leif Eriksson, became the first European to reach America in 1001.

There are a couple of contemporary accounts of these travels, but our main sources are the sagas of Iceland. The term saga *comes from the Old Norse word meaning "tale."*

Originally passed along through oral storytelling (the Vikings did not have an alphabet and could not keep written records) sagas were written down several centuries after the Viking expeditions. The most important ones were written between 1100 and 1300. The saga quoted here comes from the Vinland Sagas. Vinland, which may have meant "land of vines," is believed to be either present-day Newfoundland or New England. This translated excerpt reports the first encounter between the Vikings and the skraelings, the Norse term for the Native Americans.

TEACHING SUGGESTIONS

※ Distribute a copy of Evaluate That Document! on page 17. Ask students to consider whose point of view the sagas reflect.

※ Point out that some parts of the sagas are believed to be accurate historic records, and other parts are fanciful. Ask students to discuss whether this excerpt from the Vinland Sagas seems truthful or fanciful.

※ Tell students that *skraelings* had negative connotations for the Norse. Discuss the fact that throughout history people have often viewed outsiders negatively. Why might this be so?

※ Throughout the history of exploration, there are accounts of various "first encounters" between Native Americans and explorers. Compare and contrast these different accounts. (See pages 25, 27, 30, 39, and 40.)

※ Note that the illustration shown was made much later than the recording of the sagas. Ask students what information the illustrator might have used to create the engraving.

Map of Vinland: mid-1400s

Use with page 20.

BACKGROUND

The historic map of Vinland is the subject of enormous controversy in scholarly circles. If the map is authentic, it dates back to the mid-1400s, and offers solid support for the Norse discovery of America. At the time the map was uncovered in the 1950s, through its ultimate publication in 1965, there was strong resistance to debunking Columbus as the first explorer to reach the Americas. The controversy has been fueled by conflicting reports from laboratory analysis trying to determine the authenticity.

In fact, some historians believe that Columbus may have been aware of reports of the Viking voyages, and may have been as far north as Iceland himself prior to 1492. If the map is authentic, it provides cartographic evidence of the world view at the time, including land in what is now North America.

The upper left hand corner, labeled "Gronelada" provides a reasonable representation of Greenland. The "island of Vinland" is labeled "discovered by Bjanri and Leif." The mouths of two rivers shown may be the present-day Hudson Strait and the Gulf of St. Lawrence. The Latin text in the top left corner can be translated as

> By God's will, after a long voyage from the Island of Greenland to the south toward the most distant remaining parts

of the western ocean sea, sailing southward amidst the ice, the companions Bjarni and Leif Eriksson discovered a new land, extremely fertile and even having vines, the island which they named Vinland. Erik, legate of the Apostolic See and Bishop of Greenland and the neighboring regions, arrived in this truly vast and very rich land, in the name of Almighty God, in the last year of our most beloved father Paschal, remained a long time in both summer and winter and later returned northeastward toward Greenland and then proceede, in most humble obedience to the will of his superiors.

TEACHING SUGGESTIONS

✠ Use the Evaluate That Document! form (page 17) to help students analyze this map. Ask them to discuss the controversy surrounding the map's authenticity. The **discoveryschool.com** web site offers a lesson plan devoted to exploring the controversy with students, including readings representing both sides of the argument.

✠ Compare the Vinland map with a current map of the Western Hemisphere. Which areas seem accurate? Which are different? Students can draw in pencil an approximate outline of the North American coast over their copies of the Vinland map to highlight this comparison.

The Gutenberg Printing Press and the Gutenberg Bible: 1453–1455

Use with pages 21–22.

BACKGROUND

These documents help set a context for students about what was going on in the world just prior to the Age of Exploration. The printing press is one of the most important inventions in world history. Although the Chinese had invented a form of printing with movable characters in the early eleventh century, it was Johannes Gutenberg's printing press that launched the real development of printing. Gutenberg's Bible, printed from

1453-1455, is known as the first printed book. Within the next fifty years, over ten million books were printed. That figure stands in striking contrast to the number of books printed in the previous century: 50,000. The process he created went relatively unchanged until the 1800s.

The printing press helped support European exploration because it accelerated the flow of information and widened the channels through which texts were distributed. Columbus is known to have read the printed works of Marco Polo (see page 23) and other explorers. In addition, once Columbus returned, the news of his explorations could also be more widely disseminated (see page 30).

TEACHING SUGGESTIONS

✠ Gutenberg invented movable, reusable type, which could be arranged and rearranged on a tray. Prior to that, printers had to carve each page of a book into a wood block, inscribing the text backwards. Because this process was so tedious, most books were copied by hand. Students can get a sense of how difficult and time-consuming it is to carve text into a printing block by inscribing one sentence of a story into a Styrofoam tray. They should use a ballpoint pen and reverse the letters and direction of the text, so they're writing the passage backward. They can ink the tray and press paper on it to create a print.

✠ Gutenberg's Bible was also known as the 42-Line Bible. Ask students to look at the document to try to figure out why. (There were 42 lines per printed page.)

✠ Write the following statement on the chalkboard: "The Gutenberg Press was the most important technological advance in history." Ask students to argue whether or not they believe this statement is true.

✠ Point out to students that some of the most major technological advances to the printing process occurred relatively recently: the camera and the computer.

Marco Polo's Description of the World: 1298

Use with page 23.

BACKGROUND

Use this document together with the Gutenberg Bible document (page 22) to further emphasize the influence of printing on the Age of Exploration. This copy of Marco Polo's account belonged to and was very influential to Columbus almost two centuries after its first publication in 1298. Columbus's handwritten notes appear in the margins.

TEACHING SUGGESTIONS

- This copy of Marco Polo's account belonged to Columbus. Call students' attention to Columbus's handwritten notes in the margins. Distribute copies of Evaluate That Document! (page 17). Ask students to discuss why it is significant that Columbus' handwriting is in the margins of Marco Polo's account. Discuss the ways in which explorers built on the information—or misinformation—of those who explored before them. Ask how Polo's journeys may have influenced Columbus.
- Compare the way information was spread in the late 1400s with the way information is spread today. Point out that some recent expeditions to the top of Mount Everest have been broadcast over the Internet.
- Have students research Marco Polo and report back to the class with information about his journeys. To get started with their research, they can read a biography of Marco Polo at **http://geography.about.com**.
- Have students fill out an Explorer Collector Card for Marco Polo (page 45) and trace his route to China on a world map.

> **Answer key for Ptolemy's World Map (page 46)**
> 1. Three: Europe, Asia, and Africa;
> 2. Pacific and Arctic oceans; 3. Ultima Thule;
> 4. True; 5. Columbus must have thought the distance between the west coast of Europe and the east coast of Asia was much smaller than it actually is. That would add to his confusion about where he ended up.

Ptolemy's Geography: 1482

Use with page 24.

BACKGROUND

This map is widely used to represent the Age of Exploration. Printed in an early edition of Ptolemy's Geography *from a woodcut made in 1486, this map guided many European explorers who hoped to reach distant lands. Yet these explorers were working off a map more than 1500 years old! This fifteenth-century version was based on a map drawn in 127 A.D. by Claudius Ptolemy, a Greek scientist working in Alexandria, Egypt at the time. His books covered a vast range of topics, including astronomy, astrology, music, optics, and geography.*

While accurate in places, this map is full of errors by present-day standards. Some of the errors led Columbus to believe that the shortest route to China was westward. And partly because of this map, Columbus believed he had landed in Asia when he really landed in the West Indies.

TEACHING SUGGESTIONS

- This map uses lines of latitude and longitude. Discuss this global grid system with students using a map today. Point out that latitude could be measured accurately, but no method for accurately calculating longitude existed then. (Latitude could be calculated relatively easily from the position of the sun. But the Earth's rotation made calculating longitude difficult, particularly at sea.) The mistakes in calculating longitude were responsible for some of Columbus's erroneous assumptions.
- Distribute copies of Ptolemy's World Map (page 46), which shows a simplified version of the map on page 24. Make sure students have access to a current world map as they draw comparisons and answer the questions. The answer key is included at left.
- The first time the name "America" appeared on a map was in 1507. The name came from the explorer Amerigo Vespucci. Have students research the origin of the name "America." They can visit **http://www.americanhistory.about.com**.

COLUMBUS

Santa Fe Capitulations: 1492

Use with pages 25–26.

BACKGROUND

This document spells out the agreement between Columbus and the Spanish monarchs (Isabella and Ferdinand) for the terms of Columbus's first voyage. The documents were signed in the city of Santa Fe de Granada, Spain.

At the top of the page, the signatures read Yo el Rey *and* Yo la Reina: *"I the King" and "I the Queen." As the agreement details, Columbus was to receive one-tenth of all goods and earnings that accrued from the new land, terms which were later subject to great dispute. The agreement also ceded many titles to Columbus and his heirs.*

Columbus took the original document with him on his first voyage and upon his return it was housed in a monastery, but is currently lost. A file copy, kept in the archive of the Crown of Aragon in Barcelona, is shown here.

This document became the format for most later exploration agreements.

TEACHING SUGGESTIONS

❖ This agreement was fairly simple, granting Columbus (referred to as *Don Cristóbal Colón* in the document) almost everything he wanted. Nevertheless, the agreement took three months to prepare—in part because no one at the time realized how important the enterprise was to become. Discuss the terms of the agreement with the class. Ask them to restate them in simpler language.

❖ The agreement provides for Columbus and his heirs to receive one-tenth of "all and every kind of merchandise" accrued from the new land. Encourage students to imagine how wealthy Columbus's heirs would be today had the agreement held over time. Point out to students that the gross domestic product today is over $10 trillion. What's ten percent of that? More than $1 trillion!

The Log of Columbus: 1492

Use with pages 27–29.

BACKGROUND

When Christopher Columbus and his crew of 90 sailors began their first voyage, they were not attempting to discover America. They were searching for a route to Asia for purely economic reasons. He was searching for a foothold in the lucrative spice trade of the Far East. He hoped to find a route that would allow Europeans to barter for Asian spices of the East without going through intermediaries in Africa.

When Columbus reached the Caribbean island of San Salvador, he believed he had reached the East Indies, near Japan or China. He died in Spain still believing that he had reached Asia.

Fortunately, Columbus kept a journal of his voyage. In the introduction, he wrote: "I decided to write down everything that I might do and see and experience on this voyage, from day to day, and very carefully."

True to his resolve, Columbus kept what was by far the most detailed account of any exploration up to that time. Although his original journal was lost, the Spanish priest Bartolome de Las Casas wrote a detailed abstract of it. That abstract is now known as his journal.

Many myths about Columbus's voyage have been shattered in recent decades. Students are no longer taught that Columbus "discovered America." People know that the arrival of the European explorers was in many ways a tragedy for the Native Americans living here. However, one clear fact remains. Columbus was an exceptional seafarer. His voyages mark the beginning of the modern world.

TEACHING SUGGESTIONS

❖ Examine the point of view reflected in Columbus's journal, using the Evaluate That Document! form.

❖ Stage a debate between one group representing a Native American viewpoint and another representing the Spanish and Portuguese viewpoint. Write the following statement on the chalkboard: *Christopher Columbus is a great hero.* Encourage students to react to that statement, supporting their opinions with facts. For background and opinions about Columbus's historical role, students can visit the Kids Domain web site at **http://www.kidsdomain.com/holiday/columbusday.html**.

✠ On a playground pavement, use chalk to draw the dimensions of the three ships, the *Santa Maria,* the *Pinta,* and the *Nina,* given below. Have students stand in the ships, in numbers matching the size of the crews. (If there is not enough room, have students draw scale models on chart paper or posterboard.)
Santa Maria: 82 feet long, 28 feet wide, crew of 40; *Pinta:* 78 feet long, 26 feet wide, crew of 26; *Nina:* 74 feet long, 24 feet wide, crew of 24.

✠ Discuss what is symbolized in Columbus's coat of arms which was received in a ceremony upon his return in 1502. This coat of arms (shown on page 27) features a castle, a serpent or dragon, a group of islands, and a group of anchors. Have students create their own coats of arms. Ask them to explain what is symbolized by their images.

✠ Distribute copies of the Explorers Glossary (page 47) and Explorers Journal (page 48) and ask students to write an entry as if they were on Columbus's voyage. Encourage them to incorporate some of the navigation terms. As they encounter unfamiliar words in the documents, students can find their definitions and add them to this glossary.

Reporting on the Voyage: 1493

Use with page 30.

BACKGROUND

When Columbus returned from his first voyage, he wrote a letter to Luis de Santangel, Treasurer to the Spanish crown. De Santangel had been a strong supporter of Columbus when he was obtaining approval for his voyage.

The document fell into the hands of a printer, and was rapidly and widely disseminated through Europe. The spread of this information marked the difference between Columbus's voyage and earlier explorations; the account spurred other European countries to launch their own expeditions to the New World.

TEACHING SUGGESTIONS

✠ Using the Evaluate That Document! form, discuss how the news conveyed in this letter might have affected those who read it throughout Europe.

✠ Examine the document for truth, exaggeration, and bias. Discuss Columbus's portrayal of Native Americans. Encourage students to read *Encounter* by Jane Yolen (Harcourt, 1996), for a look at the arrival of Europeans from the Taino perspective.

✠ The beginning of this document describes the Native Americans' willingness to give things to the explorers. Columbus writes that he forbade his men to take advantage of this willingness by trading unfairly. Ask students to try to read between the lines. Were the Native Americans being taken advantage of? Were fair trades being made? What makes a trade fair and what determines the value of the exchanged items to different parties?

THE AGE OF EXPLORATION

The Sea of Darkness: 1555

Use with page 31.

BACKGROUND

Many explorers believed that the seas were full of monsters. This woodcut, from Olaus Magnus, published in 1555, is one of many depictions of the time. Although the image is imaginary, the fears were very real. Even without sea monsters, ocean travel was indeed dangerous. Perils included storms, poor navigation equipment, bad food, and ships that relied solely on wind power.

TEACHING SUGGESTIONS

- ❖ Using Evaluate That Document! (page 17), ask students to describe how explorers may have viewed the sea, according to this illustration.
- ❖ Ask students to draw their own image of what sailing the ocean might be like for them today.
- ❖ Ask students to discuss what gives the illustration its sense of foreboding. For example, direct their attention to the use of scale—the size of the serpent compared to the size of the ship. Point out that you see only the crew's bodies, another disturbing image. The serpent is both in front of and behind the ship, encompassing it. The sky and the water are one continuous gray background.

Tools of the Trade: 1602, 1700

Use with pages 32–33.

BACKGROUND

At the time of Columbus's voyage there were two main methods of naviagation available. The first was celestial navigation. That required mariners to use an astrolabe or cross staff to measure changes in their position relative to the sun or stars.

The astrolabe, first mentioned in the A.D. 900s, was used to determine latitude by measuring the angle above the horizon of either the North Star or the sun. Navigators suspended an astrolabe from a cord so that it would hang perpendicular to sea level. Then they sighted the sun or star through two small holes in the plate on its movable vane. The altitude of the celestial body could then be read on the scale around the astrolabe's rim. The cross staff relied on trigonometry to achieve the same goal. The navigator moved the cross bar until the lower limb of the cross rested on the horizon and the upper limb rested on the celestial object. The resulting reading on the cross staff allowed the navigator to triangulate his position.

The second major method of navigation was known as dead-reckoning. With dead-reckoning, the ship's pilot estimated the ship's speed by measuring the number of knots pulled off a reel by a floating log within a minute, which was timed with a sand glass. Combining

this with the direction shown on a compass helped to chart progress.

These tools offered fifteenth-century navigators improvements over older, imprecise, and (by modern standards) unscientific methods, including "measurements" taken on the lead line (an anchor which was dropped to measure distance in terms of depth and debris collected), the flight of birds, wave patterns, and the direction and speed of floating debris.

TEACHING SUGGESTIONS

- ❖ It may be difficult for your students to understand how few tools were available for navigation at the time of Columbus's voyage and subsequent European exploration. Discuss the tools that sailors use today, and compare them with what was available at the time.
- ❖ Ask students to use the information from their own research and drawings of navigational devices to create a pictorial time line of navigation advances.
- ❖ Students can visit StudyWorks online **http://www.studyworksonline.com/cda/content/explorations/0,,NAV2-5_SEP118,00.shtml** for a history of sea navigation time line. For more contemporary navigation tools, suggest that students visit the Boat Safe Kids site at **www.boatsafe.com/kids/navigation.htm**.

Treaty of Tordesillas: 1494

Use with page 34.

BACKGROUND

With the news of Columbus's explorations, Pope Alexander VI feared that Spain and Portugal would soon be at conflict over the ownership of the newly claimed lands.

After the Pope issued several Bulls (or decrees) to resolve the matter, Spain and Portugal signed the Treaty of Tordesillas in June 1494. The treaty was named after the Spanish town where it was signed.

The treaty stated that a line would be drawn, running north and south 370 leagues west of the Cape Verde Islands, off the west coast of Africa. All lands lying to the west of this line would belong to Spain. Those lying to the east would belong to Portugal. That line falls close to 50 degrees west longitude.

This agreement would enable Spain to claim the majority of land in the Americas, and, eventually, to build an empire which would stretch from the southern tip of South America to the present-day midwestern region of the United States.

Portugal also received its reward: the eastern edge of South America. This became the basis for Portugal's vast empire in Brazil.

The Treaty of Tordesillas and the bulls issued by Pope Alexander VI are among the earliest diplomatic documents of America.

TEACHING SUGGESTIONS

✠ What does the treaty reveal about Spain and Portugal's view of the world and of their role in the world? Have students complete a copy of Evaluate That Document! (page 17).

✠ Have students read the translation of the Treaty of Tordesillas and describe the agreement in their own words.

✠ Have students draw a line on a map showing how the world was to be divided. Prompt them to use the distance measurements given in the Treaty to estimate the location of the boundary line (1 league = 3 miles) and label the Spanish and Portugese "territories." You can find an online map showing where the Treaty divided the world at **http://geography.miningco.com/library/weekly/aa112999a.htm**.

Blessed Be the Light of Day: late 1400s–early 1500s

Use with page 35.

BACKGROUND

Life on board the ships was extremely difficult and dangerous. It was also sometimes boring, with each day sliding into the next against a vast, blank horizon. Sailors often filled the silence of the days with music. On many ships, including Columbus's, a boy would sing a religious song to mark the passage of each phase of the day.

TEACHING SUGGESTIONS

✠ Work with a music teacher to try to recreate the song shown. Have students practice humming the tune. They might set their own lyrics to it, as described in the third activity.

✠ The sheet music shown reads:

Salve, Regina, mater misericordiae,
Vita, dulcedo, et spes nostra, salve!

The translation is:

Hail, O Queen, mother of mercy,
Hail, our life, our sweetness and our hope!

Point out that the lyrics are recorded in Latin because these songs came from the ritual chants and songs of the Catholic church. Though the seafarers were familiar with the original songs, they adapted the lyrics for life at sea. This is reflected in the lyrics excerpted on page 35. Ask students to find the parts of the lyrics that relate specifically to their voyages.

✠ Encourage students to write some verses of their own depicting life at sea. Have them write from the perspective of a sixteenth-century sailor.

Magellan's Voyage Around the World: 1519

Use with page 36.

BACKGROUND

Ferdinand Magellan was a Portuguese seafarer. Like Columbus before him, Magellan sought a shorter route to the Indies. Like Columbus, he was looking for a western route to the Spice Islands (off of present-day Indonesia).

In 1519, Magellan left Spain with five ships and more than 200 men. He sailed past Africa, and on to South America. Magellan discovered a route of 350 miles that led from the Atlantic to the Pacific Ocean. This passage is now called the Strait of Magellan. By that time, one ship had been lost and one had returned to Europe.

The remaining ships continued for several months, until they reached Guam. Several men had died, and Magellan himself was later killed during a fight in the Philippines. His crew continued, and eventually reached Spain.

Only 18 people had survived the entire journey. These sailors were the first to circumnavigate the world.

One of these men was Antonio Pigafetta. The excerpt on page 36 is taken from Pigafetta's journal entitled The Voyage Around the World by Magellan.

TEACHING SUGGESTIONS

✠ Distribute copies of Evaluate That Document! (page 17) and discuss who authored the journal. Let students know that Magellan and 40 of his crew were killed in 1521 in a battle with local people living in the Philippines. Pigafetta escaped and his journal was published two years after he returned under Magellan's name. Ask students why he might have used Magellan as a pseudonym.

✠ Direct students' attention to the sentence, "But some others, more mindful of their honor than of their own life, determined to go to Spain alive or dead." Discuss the concept of honor in that sentence. Why might the explorers have viewed the voyage as a point of honor?

✠ On a world map, help students track Magellan's route from Portugal, around the Cape of Good Hope, and back. Encourage students to locate places mentioned in the excerpt, including the Cape of Good Hope, Antarctic Pole, and Mozambique.

✠ Distribute the Explorers Collector Cards (page 45) and ask students to fill in information about Magellan.

Salazar's Voyage: 1573

Use with page 37.

BACKGROUND

Eugenio de Salazar was a Spanish sailor who sailed across the Atlantic in 1573. Although eight decades had passed since Columbus's first voyage, the trip was still grueling. His letter to Miranda de Ron provides a vivid account of life aboard a ship.

TEACHING SUGGESTIONS

✠ Ask students to discuss the conditions described, using the Evaluate That Document! form. Based on the conditions described in this account, would they be willing to make the journey? What might have compelled men to join the crew for long journeys with uncertain outcomes?

✠ Ask students to research other working and living conditions aboard an explorer's ship. What were the different jobs? What food was served? Distribute copies of the Explorers Journal (page 48) and ask students to write their own journal entry describing life aboard an explorer's ship.

✠ Distribute copies of the Explorers Glossary (page 47) and Explorers Journal (page 48) and ask students to write an entry as if they were on Salazar's voyage. Salazar uses analogies, exaggeration, and irony. Solicit examples of these figures of speech and invite students to use similar literary devices in their journal entries.

Cabeza de Vaca's *La Relación:* 1542

Use with pages 38–39.

BACKGROUND

Alvar Nuñez Cabeza de Vaca was a Spanish explorer. In 1528 he accompanied the expedition of Pánfilo de Narváez, serving as his treasurer. The expedition landed in Florida. After a series of battles with Indians, the Spanish decided to abandon their stakes in Florida. They built five ships from the hides of horses. Most of the remaining crew died at sea, hoping to reach New Spain.

Some survivors, including de Vaca, were captured by Native Americans in Texas. Once released, de Vaca befriended the Native Americans and eventually walked across Texas, New Mexico, Arizona, and possibly part of California. In 1536 he reached present-day Mexico City. When de Vaca returned to Spain he wrote his story in a book called La Relación.

Tales of de Vaca's journey and of the wealth in what is now the southern United States inspired two other great explorers: Francisco Coronado and Hernando de Soto.

TEACHING SUGGESTIONS

✠ Using copies of Evaluate That Document! (page 17), compare the view of de Vaca's encounter with Native Americans with other accounts of encounters from other explorers (see pages 18, 25, 27, 30, 39, and 40).

✠ Using a world map, have students find the route of de Vaca's long trek. Ask them to include the exploration routes of Coronado and de Soto as well.

✠ Distribute copies of Explorers Collector Cards (page 45) and ask students to fill in the page for de Vaca, Cornonado, and de Soto.

Roanoke, the Lost Colony: 1590

Use with page 40.

BACKGROUND

In 1587, Captain John White helped settle a group of about one hundred colonists on Roanoke Island in present-day North Carolina. White sailed to England for supplies, but the Spanish War delayed his return to Roanoke. By the time he returned in 1590, the island was deserted. The fate of the Roanoke colony is still a mystery being debated by historians. White kept a detailed, illustrated log. He also created hand-drawn maps. His log is a valuable record of the surroundings and Native Americans, as well as of the colonists' experiences.

TEACHING SUGGESTIONS

✠ The excerpt from John White's log describes his return to Roanoke Island in 1590. Ask students to analyze White's view of the Native Americans, using the Evaluate That Document! form.

✠ Distribute copies of the Explorers Journal (page 48) and ask students to write an entry in their own words describing what White found when he returned to Roanoke.

✠ In this excerpt, White is looking for clues about where his men are. Make a two-column chart. Label the left column *Clues* and the right column *Conclusions*. Have the class look for clues in the passage, such as the letters CRO. In the second column discuss what conclusions White drew from the clues.

✠ Have students research and debate the mystery of Roanoke. What do they believe happened to the colonists? What can they determine about their relationship with the Native Americans? For more information about Roanoke Island, students can visit **http://www.kidinfo.com/ American_History/Colonization_Roanoke. html**.

LIFE AFTER CONTACT

Bartolome de Las Casas' *The Tears of the Indians: 1542*

Use with pages 41–42.

BACKGROUND

Bartolome de Las Casas traveled for Spain to an encomienda in Hispaniola (present-day Haiti and the Dominican Republic) in 1502. Encomiendas were tracts of Native American land granted to Spanish settlers. The Native Americans on that land were forced to work for the Spanish settlers, accept Spain as their rulers, and practice the Catholic religion.

In 1511, Las Casas experienced a revelation that made him renounce the encomienda system. He gave up his own settlement, freed the enslaved people, and began a crusade to abolish the system. In 1542 he wrote A Brief Account of the Destruction of the Indies, *describing the horrible treatment of Native Americans. It was printed ten years later and helped shape a change in policies.*

The version excerpted here is from a translation in 1656 called The Tears of the Indians.

TEACHING SUGGESTIONS

✠ Using copies of Evaluate That Document! (page 17) have students analyze the document for point of view. What makes Las Casas' point of view unusual?

✠ Make a Compare and Contrast chart with *Native Americans* on one column and *Spaniards* on the other. Pick out adjectives and phrases from the excerpt that describe each group. Discuss how those words reflect point of view.

❖ Compare the *encomienda* system with the enslavement of Africans.

Smallpox: late 1500s

Use with page 43.

BACKGROUND

The European explorers brought contagious diseases with them to the Americas. Having been exposed to them before, the Europeans had built up immunities and were not threatened. However, the Native Americans had no resistance to the new germs carried across the ocean. Diseases such as smallpox, measles, and typhoid fever killed thousands of Native Americans. By 1650, smallpox had killed 75 percent of North American Native Americans.

This Aztec codex, a historical record written in pictographs comes from a document called the Florentine Codex and shows the effects of the smallpox epidemic among the Aztecs. The arrival of Cortés in 1519 in Mexico marked the beginning of exposure of the Aztecs and other groups to European diseases.

TEACHING SUGGESTIONS

❖ The Florentine Codex (more formally known as the *General History of the Things of New Spain*) contains illustrations and notations drawn by Aztecs. The project was collected and supervised by a Franciscan monk, Bernardo de Sahagun in the 1500s. Consisting of twelve volumes, it has been a major resource for scholars attempting to research the Aztec point of view. Recently, there has been controversy about relying on this document, and questions have been raised about the point of view. Does it truly represent the Aztec viewpoint? or is it the colonists' view of the Aztec viewpoint? Distribute the Evaluate That Document! analysis sheet (page 17) to students, to discuss the point of view shown in this illustration. Students can visit **http://www.finns-books.com/florent.htm** to view this illustration and others from the Florentine Codex.

❖ The illustration shows one medicine woman tending to five women with smallpox. The speech scrolls, or balloons, indicate speech. Ask students to write captions for what the medicine woman might be saying. The woman below appears to be calling out for her. What might she be saying?

❖ Read the following statement to students and ask them to agree or disagree (they may want to conduct research to support their answers): *The spread of smallpox in North America was a form of germ warfare.*

❖ Discuss the fact that the spread of smallpox has been curbed because of vaccines. Students may be aware, however, that smallpox has become a potential threat again. Depending on your students' ages, sensitivity, and awareness of the news, you may want to let them discuss what they know about the possibility of smallpox being used as a terrorist weapon. Encourage them to research how vaccines are being produced to meet such a threat.

Evaluate That Document!

Title or name of document _____

Date of document _____

Type of document:

- ❑ letter
- ❑ diary/journal
- ❑ newspaper article
- ❑ photograph
- ❑ map
- ❑ telegram

- ❑ patent
- ❑ poster
- ❑ advertisement
- ❑ drawing/painting
- ❑ cartoon
- ❑ other _____

Point of View:

Who created this document? _____

For whom was this document created? _____

_____

What was the purpose for creating this document? _____

_____

What might the person who created it have been trying to express? _____

_____

What are two things you can learn about the time period from this primary source?

_____

_____

What other questions do you have about this source?

_____

_____

_____

_____

_____

_____

The Vinland Sagas

c. 1000 A.D.

The Mariners Museum

The first winter passed into summer, and then they had their first encounter with Skraelings, when a great number of them came out of the woods one day. The cattle were grazing near by and the bull began to bellow and roar with great vehemence. This terrified the Skraelings and they fled, carrying their packs which contained furs and sables and pelts of all kinds. They made for Karlsefni's houses and tried to get inside, but Karlsefni had the doors barred against them. Neither side could understand the other's language.

Then the Skraeings put down their packs and opened them up and offered their contents, preferably in exchange for weapons; but Karlsefni forbade his men to sell arms. Then he hit on the idea of telling the women to carry milk out to the Skraeings, and when the Skraelings saw the milk they wanted to buy nothing else. And so the outcome of their trading expedition was that the Skraelings carried their purchases away in their bellies, and left their packs and furs with Karlsefni and his men.

After that, Karlsefni ordered a strong wooden palisade to be erected round the houses, and they settled in.

About this time Karlsefni's wife, Gudrid, gave birth to a son, and he was named Snorri.

Early next winter the Skraelings returned, in much greater numbers this time, bringing with them the same kind of wares as before. Karlsefni told the women, 'You must carry out to them the same produce that was most in demand last time, and nothing else.'

As soon as the Skraelings saw it they threw their packs in over the palisade.

Scholastic Professional Books

Gudrid was sitting in the doorway beside the cradle of her son Snorri when a shadow fell across the door and a woman entered wearing a black, close-fitting tunic; she was rather short and had a band round her chestnut-coloured hair. She was pale, and had the largest eyes that have ever been seen in any human head. She walked up to Gudrid and said, 'What is your name?'

'My name is Gudrid. What is yours?'

'My name is Gudrid,' the woman replied.

Then Gudrid, Karlsefni's wife, motioned to the woman to come and sit beside her; but at that very moment she heard a great crash and the woman vanished, and in the same instant a Skraeling was killed by one of Karlsefni's men for trying to steal some weapons. The Skraelings fled as fast as they could, leaving their clothing and wares behind. No one had seen the woman except Gudrid.

'Now we must devise a plan,' said Karlsefni, 'for I expect they will pay us a third visit, and this time with hostility and in greater numbers. This is what we must do: ten men are to go out on the headland here and make themselves conspicuous, and the rest of us are to go into the wood and make a clearing there, where we can keep our cattle when the Skraelings come out of the forest. We shall take our bull and keep him to the fore.'

The place where they intended to have their encounter with the Skraelings had the lake on one side and the woods on the other.

Karlsefni's plan was put into effect, and the Skraelings came right to the place that Karlsefni had chosen for the battle. The fighting began, and many of the Skraelings were killed. There was one tall and handsome man among the Skraelings and Karlsefni reckoned that he must be their leader. One of the Skraelings had picked up an axe, and after examining it for a moment he swung it at a man standing beside him, who fell dead at once. The tall man then took hold of the axe, looked at it for a moment, and then threw it as far as he could out into the water. Then the Skraelings fled into the forest as fast as they could, and that was the end of the encounter.

Karlsefni and his men spent the whole winter there, but in the spring he announced that he had no wish to stay there any longer and wanted to return to Greenland. They made ready for the voyage and took with them much valuable produce, vines and grapes and pelts. They put to sea and reached Eiriksfjord safely and spent the winter there.

Excerpt from *The Vinland Sagas*, translated by Magnus Magnusson and Hermann Palsson

Map of Vinland

mid-1400s

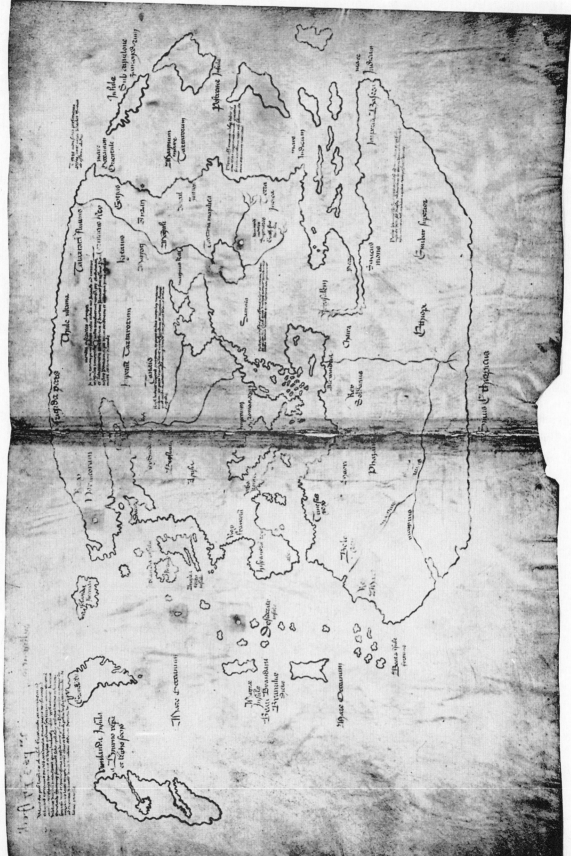

The Gutenberg Printing Press
1453

North Wind Picture Archives

North Wind Picture Archives

The Gutenberg Bible

1453–1455

North Wind Picture Archives

Marco Polo's Description of the World

1298 (printed edition with notes from Columbus late 1400's)

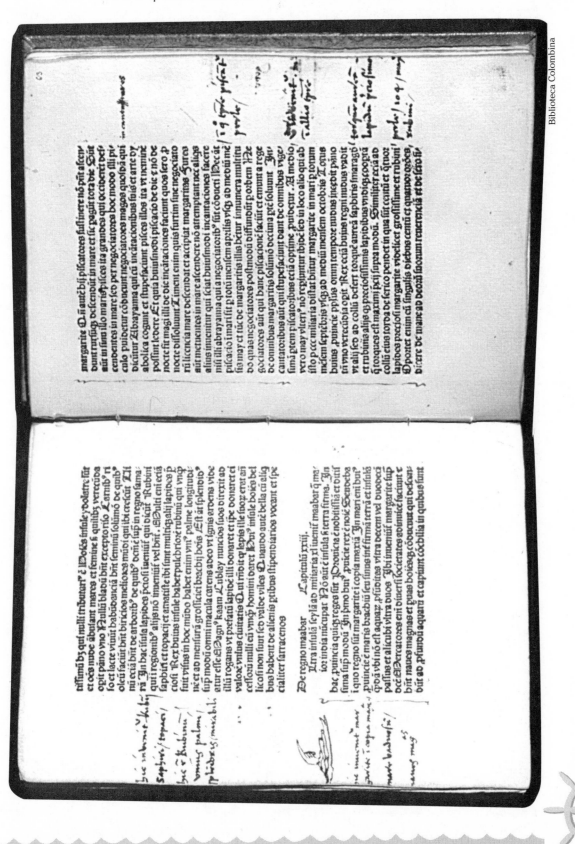

Ptolemy's Geography
1482

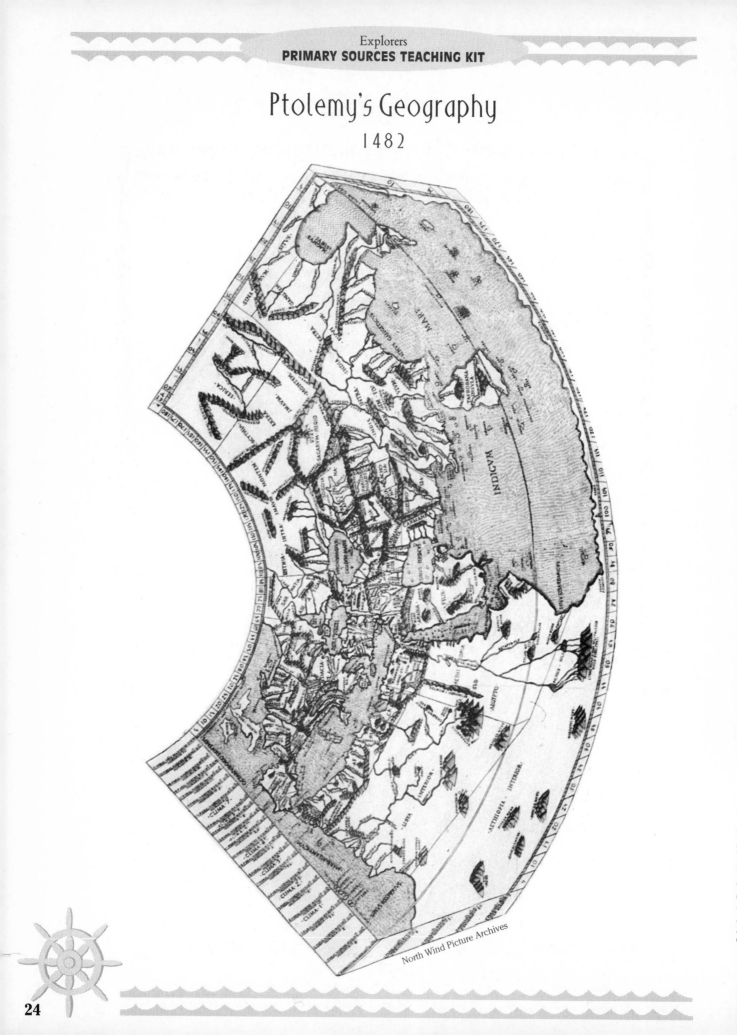

North Wind Picture Archives

Santa Fe Capitulations

Archivo General de Indias, Seville

The things prayed for, and which Your Highnesses give and grant to Don Cristóbal Colón as some recompense for what he is to discover in the Oceans, and for the voyages which now, with the help of God, he has engaged to make therein in the service of your Highnesses, are the following:

Firstly, that Your Highnesses, as actual Lords of the said Oceans, appoint from this date the said Don Cristóbal Colón to be your Admiral in all those islands and mainlands which by his activity and industry shall be discovered or acquired in the said oceans, during his lifetime, and likewise, after his death, his heirs and successors one after another in perpetuity, with all the preeminences and prerogatives appertaining to the said office . . .

Likewise, that Your Highnesses appoint the said Don Cristóbal Colón to be your Viceroy and Governor General in all the said island and mainlands . . .

Item, that of all and every kind of merchandise, whether pearls, precious stones, gold, silver, spices, and other objects and merchandise whatsoever, of whatever kind, name and sort, which may be bought, bartered, discovered, acquired and obtained within the limits of the said Admiralty, Your Highnesses grant from now henceforth to the said Don Cristóbal, and will that he may have and take for himself, the tenth part of the whole . . .

The Log of Columbus
1492

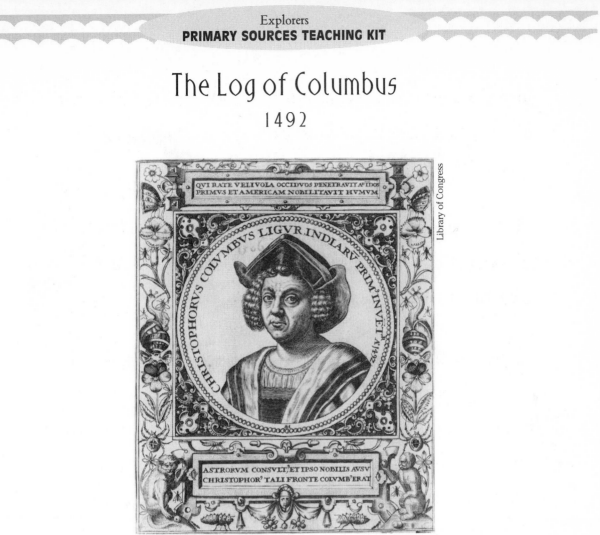

Library of Congress

Friday, 3 August 1492. Set sail from the bar of Saltes at 8 o'clock, and proceeded with a strong breeze till sunset, . . . or fifteen leagues south, afterwards southwest and south by west, which is the direction of the Canaries.

Monday, 6 August. The rudder of the caravel Pinta became loose, being broken or unshipped. It was believed that this happened by the contrivance of Gomez Rascon and Christopher Quintero, who were on board the caravel, because they disliked the voyage. Made a progress, day and night, of twenty-nine leagues.

Sunday, 9 September. Sailed this day nineteen leagues, and determined to count less than the true number, that the crew might not be dismayed if the voyage should prove long. In the night sailed one hundred and twenty miles, at the rate of ten miles an hour, which make thirty leagues. The sailors steered badly, causing the vessels to fall to leeward toward the northeast, for which the Admiral reprimanded them repeatedly.

The Log of Columbus

King Ferdinand

Queen Isabella

Sunday, 16 September. Sailed day and night, west thirty-nine leagues, and reckoned only thirty-six. Some clouds arose and it drizzled . . . Here they began to meet with large patches of weeds very green, and which appeared to have been recently washed away from the land; on which account they all judged themselves to be near some island, though not a continent, according to the opinion of the Admiral, who says, "the continent we shall find further ahead."

Thursday, 11 October. Steered west-southwest; and encountered a heavier sea than they had met with before in the whole voyage. Saw pardelas and a green rush near the vessel. The crew of the Pinta saw a cane and a log; they also picked up a stick which appeared to have been carved with an iron tool, a piece of cane, a plant which grows on land, and a board. The crew of the Nina saw other signs of land, and a stalk loaded with rose berries. These signs encouraged them, and they all grew cheerful. Sailed this day till sunset, twenty-seven leagues.

The Admiral again perceived [land] once or twice, appearing like the light of a wax candle moving up and down, which some thought an indication of land. But the Admiral held it for certain that land was near; for which reason, after they had said the Salve which the seamen are accustomed to repeat and chant after their fashion, the Admiral directed them to keep a strict watch upon the forecastle and look out diligently for land, and to him who should first discover it he promised a silken jacket, besides the reward which the King and Queen had offered, which was an annuity of ten thousand maravedis.

Scholastic Professional Books

The Log of Columbus

North Wind Picture Archives

At two o'clock in the morning the land was discovered, at two leagues' distance . . . Presently they described people, naked, and the Admiral landed in the boat, which was armed, along with Martin Alonzo Pinzon, and Vincent Yanez his brother, captain of the Nina. The Admiral bore the royal standard, and the two captains each a banner of the Green Cross, which all the ships had carried; this contained the initials of the names of the King and Queen each side of the cross, and a crown over each letter. Arrived on shore, they saw trees very green, many streams of water, and diverse sorts of fruits. The Admiral called upon the two Captains, and the rest of the crew who landed, as also to Rodrigo de Escovedo notary of the fleet, and Rodrigo Sanchez, of Segovia, to bear witness that he before all others took possession (as in fact he did) of that island for the King and Queen his sovereigns . . . Here follow the precise words of the Admiral: "As I saw that they were very friendly to us, and perceived that they could be much more easily converted to our holy faith by gentle means than by force, I presented them with some red caps, and strings of beads to wear upon the neck, and many other trifles of small value, wherewith they were much delighted, and became wonderfully attached to us. Afterwards they came swimming to the boats, bringing parrots, balls of cotton thread, javelins, and many other things which they exchanged for articles we gave them, such as glass beads, and hawk's bells; which trade was carried on with the utmost good will. But they seemed on the whole to me, to be a very poor people."

Reporting on the Voyage

1493

EXCERPTS FROM THE LETTER OF CHRISTOPHER COLUMBUS TO LUIS DE SANTANGEL

. . . They are by nature fearful and timid. Yet when they perceive that they are safe, putting aside all fear, they are of simple manners and trustworthy, and very liberal with everything they have, refusing no one who asks for anything they may possess, and even themselves inviting us to ask for things. ❦ They show greater love for all others than for themselves; they give valuable things for trifles, being satisfied even with a very small return, or with nothing; however, I forbade that things so small and of no value should be given to them such as pieces of plates, dishes and glass, likewise keys and shoe-straps; although if they were able to obtain these, it seemed to them like getting the most beautiful jewels in the world. ❦ These people practice no

Library of Congress

kind of idolatry; on the contrary they firmly believe that all strength and power, and in fact all good things are in heaven, and that I had come down from thence with these ships and sailors; and in this belief I was received there after they had put aside fear. Nor are they slow or unskilled, but of excellent and acute understanding.... ❦ As soon as I reached that sea, I seized by force several Indians on the first island, in order that they might learn from us, and in like manner tell us about those things in these lands of which they themselves had knowledge; and the plan succeeded, for in a short time we understood them and they us, sometimes by gestures and signs, sometimes by words; and it was a great advantage to us. ❦ They are coming with me now, yet always believing that I descended from heaven, although they have been living with us for a long time, and are living with us today. And these men were the first who announced it wherever we landed, continually proclaiming to the others in a loud voice, "Come, come, and you will see the celestial people." Whereupon both women and men, both children and adults, both young men and old men, laying aside the fear caused a little before, visited us eagerly, filling the road with a great crowd, some bringing food, and some drink, with great love and extraordinary goodwill... ❦ They tell me of another island greater than the aforesaid Hispaña, whose inhabitants are without hair, and which abounds in gold above all the others. I am bringing with me men of this island and of the others that I have seen, who give proof of the things that I have described.

The Sea of Darkness
1555

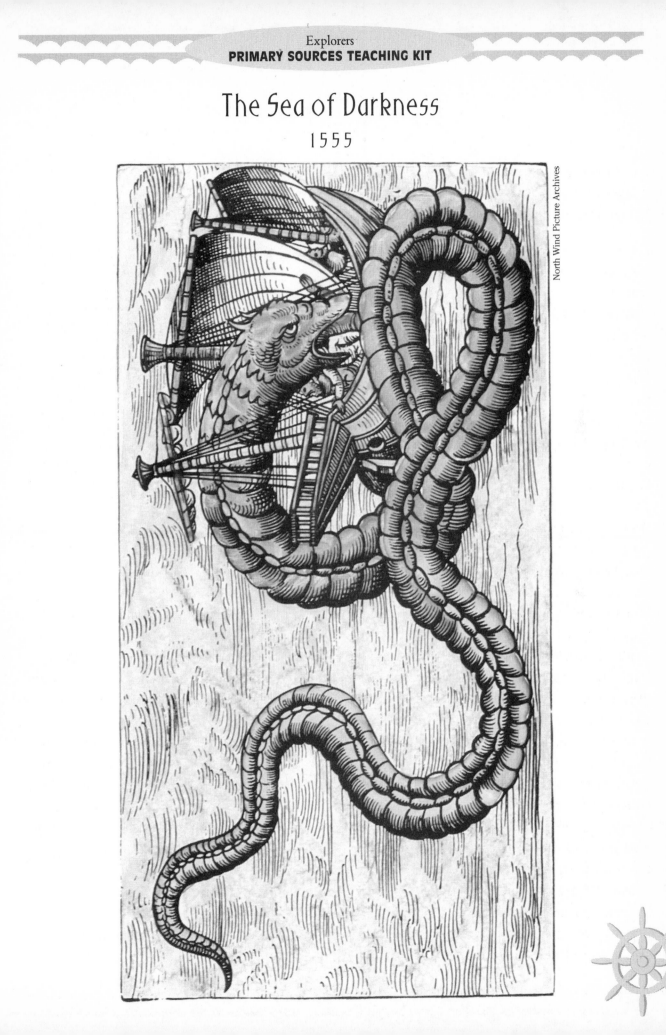

North Wind Picture Archives

Tools of the Trade
1602

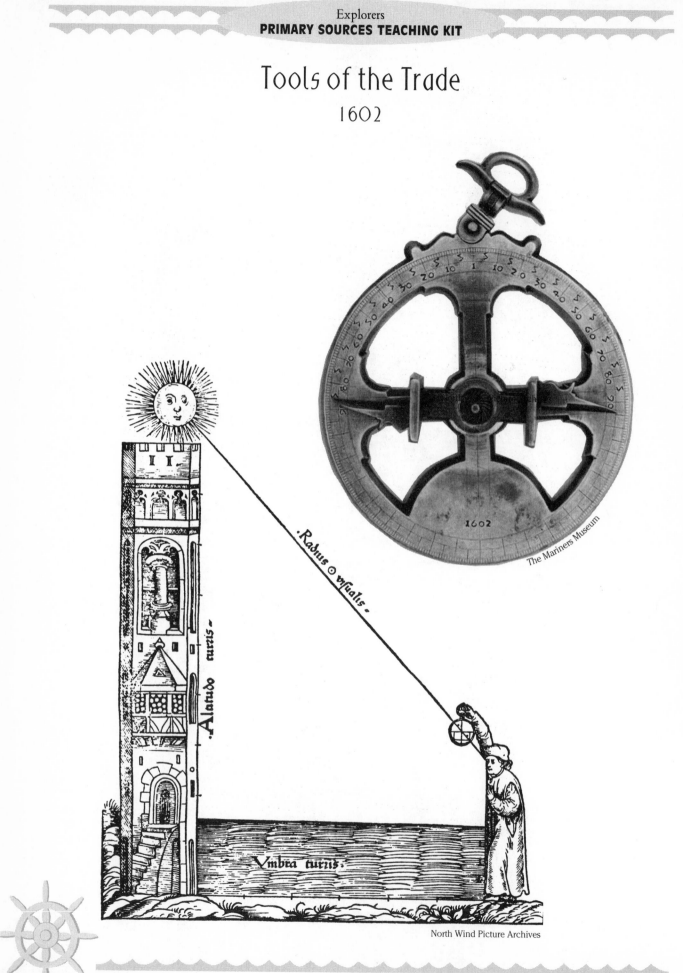

The Mariners Museum

.Radus ☉ vſualis.

·Alatudo turris·

Vmbra turris.

North Wind Picture Archives

Tools of the Trade
1700

The Mariners Museum

200   *The Use of the Cross-Staff.*

The Figure of the Cross-Staff.

The Description of the Cross-Staff.

This Instrument is of some antiquity in Navigation, and is commonly used at Sea, to take the Altitude of the Sun or Stars, which it performs with sufficient exactness, especially if it be less then 60 degrees, but if it exceed 60, it is not so certain, by reason of the length of the Cross, and the smallness of the graduations on the Staff.

The

National Maritime Museum

Treaty of Tordesillas
1494

In the name of God Almighty, Father, Son, and Holy Ghost, three truly separate and distinct persons and only one divine essence. Be it manifest and known to all who shall see this public instrument, that at the village of Tordesillas, on the seventh day of the month of June, in the year of the nativity of our Lord Jesus Christ in 1494 . . .

. . . that a boundary or straight line shall be determined and drawn north and south, from pole to pole, on the said ocean sea, from the Arctic to the Antarctic pole. This boundary or line shall be drawn straight, as aforesaid, at a distance of three hundred and seventy leagues west of the Cape Verde Islands, being calculated by degrees. . . . And all lands, both islands and mainlands, found and discovered already, or to be found and discovered hereafter, by the said

Archivo General de Indias, Seville

King of Portugal and by his vessels on this side of the said line and bound determined as above, toward the east, in either north or south latitude, on the eastern side of the said bound shall belong to, and remain in the possession of, and pertain forever to, the said King of Portugal and his successors.

And all other lands, both islands and mainlands, found or to be found hereafter, discovered or to be discovered hereafter, which have been discovered or shall be discovered by the said King and Queen of Castile, Aragon, etc., and by their vessels, on the western side of the said bound . . . shall belong to, and remain in the possession of, and pertain forever to the said King and Queen of Castile, León, etc., and to their successors . . . .

Excerpts from *Treaty of Tordesillas*

Scholastic Professional Books

Blessed Be the Light of Day

late 1400s–early 1500s

At Dawn

Blessed be the light of day
And the Holy Cross, we say;
And the Lord of Verity
And the Holy Trinity.
Blessed be th'immortal soul
And the Lord who keeps it whole,
Blessed be the light of day
And he who sends the night away.

At 6:30 A.M.

Good is that which passeth
Better that which cometh
Seven is passed and eight floweth
More shall flow if God willeth
Count and pass makes voyage fast

At Dusk

Blessed be the hour
In which God was born
Saint Mary who bore Him
Saint John who baptized Him.
The watch is called,
The glass floweth;
We shall make a good voyage if
God willeth.

At Night

One glass is gone
And now the second floweth,
More shall run down
If my God willeth.
To my God let's pray
To give us a good voyage;
And through His blessed Mother,
    our advocate on high,
Protect us from the waterspout and
    send no tempest nigh.

Houghton Library, Harvard University

Hail, O Queen, mother of mercy,

Hail, our life, our sweetness and our hope!

Lyrics from *Blessed Be the Light of Day*

Magellan's Voyage Around The World
1519

Prima ego velivolis ambivi cursibus Orbem,
Magellane novo te duce ducta freto.

The Mariners Museum

In order to round the Cape of Good Hope we went as far south as 42 degrees toward the Antarctic Pole. We remained near this Cape for seven weeks with sails furled because of the west and northwest wind on our bow, and in a very great storm.... Some of our men, both sick and healthy, wished to go to a place of the Portuguese called Mozambique, because the ship was taking in much water, and also for the great cold, and still more because we had nothing else to eat except rice and water, since for want of salt the meat which we had was rotten and putrefied. But some others, more mindful of their honor than of their own life, determined to go to Spain alive or dead.

At length, by God's help, on the sixth of May we passed this Cape at a distance of 5 leagues from it.... Then we sailed northwest for two months continually without taking any refreshment or repose. And in that short space of time twenty-one of our men died....

On Saturday the sixth of September, 1522, we entered the Bay..., and we were only 18 men, the most part sick.... From the time when we departed from that Bay until the present day we had sailed fourteen thousand four hundred and sixty leagues, and completed the circuit of the world from east to west.

—Antonio Pigafetta

Salazar's Voyage
1573

EXCERPT FROM SALAZAR'S JOURNAL

We were given, as a great privilege, a tiny cabin, about two feet by three; and packed in there, the movements of the sea upset our heads and stomachs so horribly that we all turned white as ghosts and began to bring up our very souls . . . [The ship] is a long narrow city, sharp and pointed at one end, wider at the other, like the pier of a bridge . . . the dwellings are so closed-in, dark, and evil-smelling that they seem more like burial vaults. . . . There are running rivers, not of sweet, clear, flowing water, but of turbid filth; full not of grains of gold . . . but of grains of very singular pearl—enormous lice, so big that sometimes they vomit bits of apprentice.

The ground of this city is such, that when it rains the soil is hard, but when the sun is hot the mud becomes soft and your feet stick to the ground so that you can hardly lift them. For game in the neighborhood, there are fine flights of cockroaches—and very good rat-hunting, the rats so fierce that when they are cornered they turn on the hunters like wild boars.

. . . Whenever you stand on the open deck, as sea is sure to come aboard to visit and kiss your feet; it fills your boots with water, and when they are dry they are caked with salt, so that the leather cracks and burns in the sun. If you want to walk the deck for exercise, you have to get two sailors to take your arms, like a village bride; if you don't you will end up with your feet in the air and your head in the scuppers.

North Wind Picture Archives

Cabeza de Vaca's *La Relación*
1542

CHAPTER XI
OF WHAT BEFELL LOPE DE OVIEDO WITH THE INDIANS

After the people had eaten, I ordered Lope de Oviedo, who had more strength and was stouter than any of the rest, to go to some trees that were near by, and climbing into one of them to look about and try to gain knowledge of the country. He did as I bade, and made out that we were

North Wind Picture Archives

on an island. He saw that the land was pawed up in the manner that ground is wont to be where cattle range, whence it appeared to him that this should be a country of Christians; and thus he reported to us. I ordered him to return and examine much more particularly, and see if there were any roads that were worn, but without going far, because there might be danger.

He went, and coming to a path, took it for the distance of half a league, and found some huts, without tenants, they having gone into the woods. He took from these an earthen pot, a little dog, some few mullets, and returned. As it appeared to us he was gone a long time, we sent two men that they should look to see what might have happened. They met him near by, and saw that three Indians with bows and arrows followed and were calling to him, while he, in the same way, was beckoning them on. Thus he arrived where we were, the natives remaining a little way back, seated on the shore. Half an hour after, they were supported by one hundred other Indian bowmen, who if they were not large, our fears made giants of them. They stopped near us with the first three. It were idle to think that any among us could make defence; for it would have been difficult to find six that could rise from the ground. The Assessor and I went out and called to them, and they came to us. We endeavored the best we could to encourage them and secure their favor. We gave them beads and hawk-bells, and each of them gave me an arrow, which is a pledge of friendship. They told us by signs that they would return in the morning and bring us something to eat, as at that time they had nothing.

Excerpt from *La Relación*, by Alvar Nuñez Cabeza de Vaca

Cabeza de Vaca's *La Relación*
1542

CHAPTER XII
THE INDIANS BRING US FOOD

At sunrise the next day, the time the Indians appointed, they came according to their promise, and brought us a large quantity of fish with certain roots, some a little larger than walnuts, others a trifle smaller, the greater part got from under the water and with much labor. In the evening they returned and brought us more fish and roots. They sent their women and children to look at us, who went back rich with the hawk-bells and beads given them, and they came afterwards on other days, returning as before. Finding that we had provision, fish, roots, water and other things we asked for, we determined to embark again and pursue our course. Having dug out our boat from the sand in which it was buried, it became necessary that we should strip, and go through great exertion to launch her, we being in such a state that things very much lighter sufficed to make us great labor.

Thus embarked, at the distance of two cross-bow shots in the sea we shipped a wave that entirely wet us. As we were naked, and the cold was very great, the oars loosened in our hands, and the next blow the sea struck us, capsized the boat. The Assessor and two others held fast to her for preservation, but it happened to be far otherwise; the boat carried them over, and they were drowned under her. As the surf near the shore was very high, a single roll of the sea threw the rest into the waves and half drowned upon the shore of the island, without our losing any more than those the boat took down. The survivors escaped naked as they were born, with the loss of all they had; and although the whole was of little value, at that time it was worth much, as we were then in November, the cold was severe, and our bodies were so emaciated the bones might be counted with little difficulty, having become the perfect figures of death.

Excerpt from *La Relación*, by Alvar Nuñez Cabeza de Vaca

Roanoke, the Lost Colony
1590

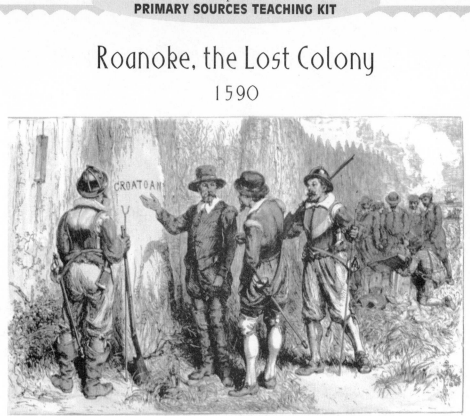

North Wind Picture Archives

From hence we went through the woods to that part of the Island. . . , until we came to the place where I left our Colony in 1586. In all this way we saw in the sand the print of the Savages, and as we entered up the sandy bank upon a tree, in the very brow thereof were curiously carved these letters C R O: which letters presently we knew to signify the place, where I should find the planters seated, according to a secret token agreed upon between them & me at my last departure from them. . . Therefore at my departure from them in 1587 I willed them, that if they should happen to be distressed in any of those places, that then they should carve over the letters or name, a Cross in this form, but we found no such sign of distress. And having well considered of this, we passed toward the place where they were left in sundry houses, but we found the houses taken down… and one of the chief trees or posts at the right side of the entrance had the bark taken off, and 5 foot from the ground was carved CROATOAN. . . Presently Captain Cooke and I went to the place, which was in the end of an old trench where we found five Chests, that had been carefully hidden of the Planters, and of the same chests three were my own, and. . . many of my things were broken, and my books torn from the covers, the frames of some of my pictures and Maps rotten and spoiled with rain, and my armor almost eaten through with rust; this could be no other but the deed of the Savages. . . , who had watched the departure of our men to Croatoan; and as soon as they were departed, digged up every place where they suspected any thing to be buried: but although it much grieved. . . I greatly joyed that I had safely found a certain token of their safe being at Croatoan.

Excerpted from John White's log, 1590

Scholastic Professional Books

Bartolome de Las Casas' *The Tears of the Indians*
1542

North Wind Picture Archives

These Countreys are inhabited by such a number of people, as if God had assembled and called together to this place, the greatest part of Mankinde. This infinite multitude of people was so created by God, as that they were without fraud, without subtilty or malice, to their natural Governours most faithful and obedient. Toward the Spaniards whom they serve, patient, meek and peaceful, and who laying all contentious and tumultuous thoughts aside, live without any hatred or desire of revenge; the people are most delicate and tender, enjoying such a freble constitution of body as does not permit them to endure labour, so that the Children of Princes and great persons here, are not more nice and delicate then the Children of the meanest Countrey-man in that place. The Nation is very poor and indigent, possessing little, and by reason that they gape not after temporal goods, neither proud nor ambitious...

Bartolome de Las Casas' *The Tears of the Indians*

To these quiet Lambs, endued with such blessed qualities, came the Spaniards like most cuel Tygres, Wolves, and Lions, enrag'd with a sharp and redious hunger; for these forty years past, minding nothing else but the slaughter of these unfortunate wretches, whom with divers kinds of torments neither seen nor heard of before, they have so cruelly and inhumanely butchered, that of three millions of people which Hispaniola it self did contain, there are left remaining alive scarce three hundred persons.

That which led the Spaniards to these unsanctified impieties was the desire of Gold, to make themselves suddenly rich, for the obtaining of dignities & honours which were no way fit for them. In a word, their covetousness, their ambition, which could not be more in any people under heaven, the riches of the Countrey, and the patience of the people gave occasion to this their devillish barbarism. . . . The Indians never gave them the least cause to offer them violence, but received them as Angels sent from heaven, till their excessive cruelties, the torments and slaughters of their Countrymen mov'd them to take Armes against the Spaniards.

From *A Brief Account of the Destruction of the Indies*, by Bartolome de Las Casas

Smallpox
late 1500s

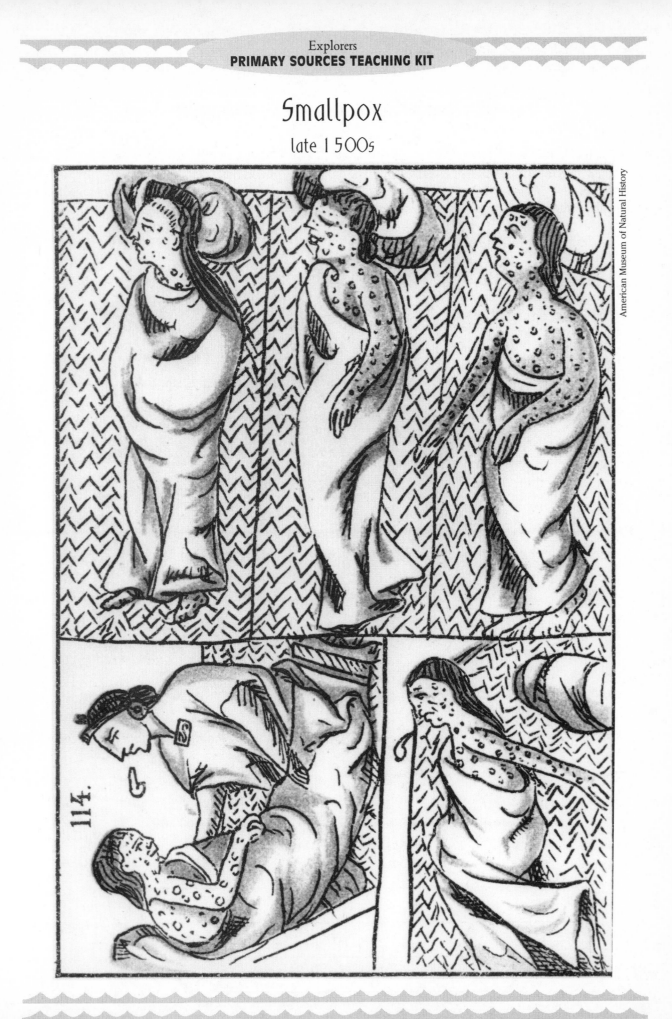

American Museum of Natural History

Explorers KWL Ship Chart

In the ship chart below, write down what you already know about the Age of Exploration or a particular explorer in the *K* box, and then write what you want to learn in the *W* box.

When you've found the answers to your questions, record your discoveries in the *L* box and new questions in the *What I still want to learn* section.

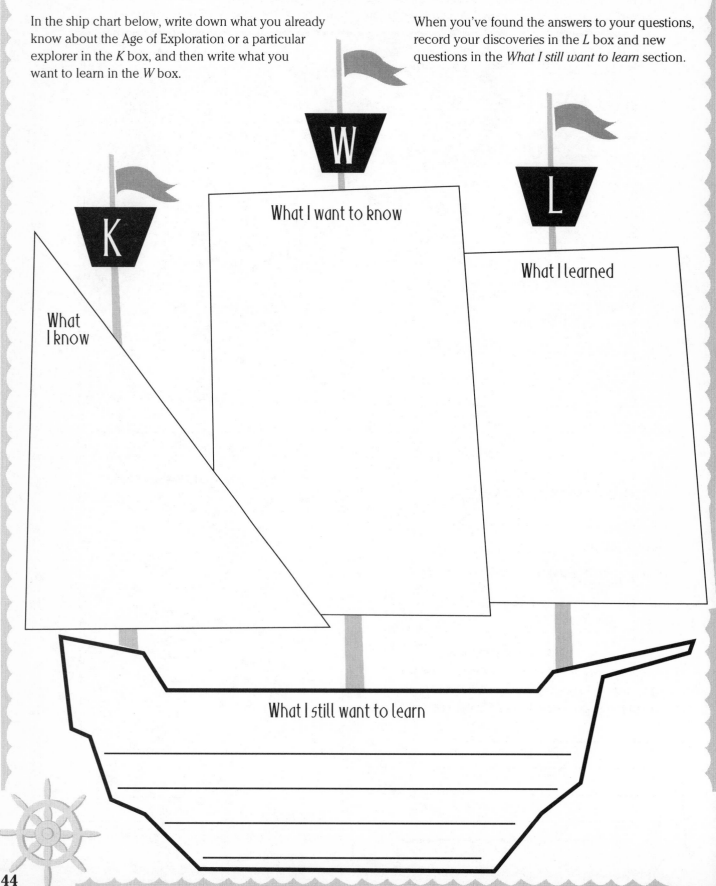

K — What I know

W — What I want to know

L — What I learned

What I still want to learn

EXPLORERS COLLECTOR CARDS

Create your own Explorer collector cards to keep track of who went where when! Collect them and trade them! Use a world map to trace the routes of each explorer. After completing the cards on the sheet, cut them out and fold back to front. Secure them with tape or glue.

Date of most important voyage:_____

_____

Area he explored:_____

Country and leaders who sponsored the voyage:

_____

_____

GOALS OF EXPLORATION

(check off the goals and give a brief explanation below)

❑ Wealth ❑ Fame ❑ National Pride

❑ Religion ❑ Foreign Goods ❑ Better Trade Routes

_____

_____

_____

_____

A portrait of the explorer

_____

Birthdate _____

Country of birth _____

Date of most important voyage:_____

_____

Area he explored:_____

Country and leaders who sponsored the voyage:

_____

_____

GOALS OF EXPLORATION

(check off the goals and give a brief explanation below)

❑ Wealth ❑ Fame ❑ National Pride

❑ Religion ❑ Foreign Goods ❑ Better Trade Routes

_____

_____

_____

_____

A portrait of the explorer

_____

Birthdate _____

Country of birth _____

Cut cards at border

Fold cards here

PTOLEMY'S WORLD MAP

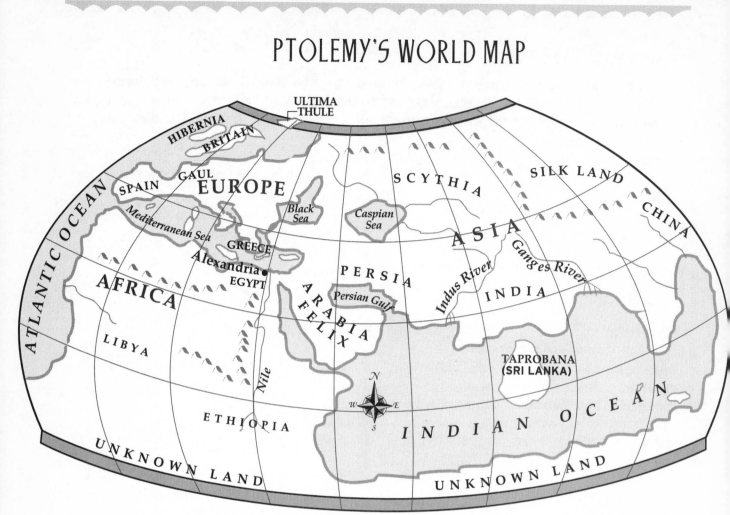

The map shown above is a simplified version of Ptolemy's map. Compare this map with a current world map to answer the questions below.

1. How many continents made up Ptolemy's "known world"?_____

2. Which two oceans did Ptolemy not include on his map?_____

3. Which island did Ptolemy consider to be the most northerly of his world?_____

4. True or false: Ptolemy made a mistake when he mapped the Indian Ocean as a landlocked sea. _____

5. Christopher Columbus used a copy of Ptolemy's map on his journey to America in 1492. How might the mistakes on the map have affected Columbus' journey?

_____

_____

_____

Adapted from "Claudius Ptolemy" in Mapman's Guide To Understanding Your World by Jim McMahon (Scholastic, 2001)

Explorers Glossary

Land ahoy! Learn some of the language of the high seas, plus other terms of the times in this glossary of exploration. Use them as you write about the explorers' experiences, as well as those who already lived here.

Ship Talk

caravel
a two- or three-masted Portuguese ship sailed in the 1400s

cartography
the study of maps

circumnavigate
to go completely around the world

conquistador
Spanish conquerors/explorers who sailed to the Americas to search for riches; they were often ruthless in their pursuit of gold and other treasures

dead reckoning
a navigation method used by Columbus that involved calculating your own speed, the speed and direction of the wind, ocean currents, and compass directions.

epidemic
a disease contracted by many people at one time

expedition
a journey made for a particular purpose

fathom
a unit of measurement of depth of the sea; a fathom is about 6 ft., the approximate span of a sailor's outstretched arms.

landfall
land sighted or reached along the voyage

navigate
to determine a ship's location and the direction and distance it traveled

Story Starter Tip!

If you choose to write a story about the experiences of an explorer or a Native American during the time of European exploration in the New World, here are some suggestions to get you started:

*The sky darkened and the calm water grew choppy. I gazed at the mast and signaled to the crew…

*A strange wooden shape was approaching the shore. It grew bigger and bigger. It rested on the water like a giant duck. But there were people on board….

*After we set up camp we began exploring the area. We soon came upon the most amazing site…

*There was enough food left, if we were careful, for three more days. After that, I wasn't sure what we would do…

*At first we were frightened by the new people. They looked very different from us. We soon learned that they could teach us so much. And we could teach them too…

Name

Explorers Journal